A WOMAN'S HEART

GOD'S DWELLING PLACE

LEADER GUIDE

Beth Moore

LifeWay Press®
Nashville, Tennessee

About the Author

Judi Slayden Hayes is a writer and an editor. She and her husband David live in Mt. Juliet, Tennessee, with their cat, Chapel. They are members of First Baptist Church, Nashville. Judi loves to travel and has visited 37 countries on five continents. Whether on the road or at home, she always has a pile of books to read.

ISBN 978-1-4158-5579-9
Item 005077200

Dewey Decimal Classification: 220.07
Subject heading: BIBLE STUDY \ WOMEN—RELIGIOUS LIFE \
STUDY AND TEACHING

To order additional copies of this resource: WRITE LifeWay Church Resources Customer Service; One LifeWay Plaza; Nashville, TN 37234-0113; FAX order to (615) 251-5933; CALL toll-free 1-800-458-2772; E-MAIL *orderentry@lifeway.com*; ORDER ONLINE at *www.lifeway.com*; or VISIT the LifeWay Christian Store serving you.

Printed in the United States of America

Leadership and Adult Publishing
LifeWay Church Resources
One LifeWay Plaza
Nashville, TN 37234-0175

Contents

Introduction

A Woman's Heart: God's Dwelling Place is an in-depth study of the Old Testament tabernacle. This study is based on two vital themes:

- A holy God's persistent desire to dwell among His people
- God's invitation for us to pass through the distant courts of our relationships with Him and to enter the intimacy of the holy of holies

This guide will equip you to plan and lead a study of *A Woman's Heart* for women in your church or community. In it you will find a retreat plan for launching the study, help for planning and promoting the study, and a session-by-session guide with ideas for conducting the study. The study consists of an introductory session and 10 weeks of group-study sessions for a total of 11 weeks. The study offers a combination of daily, individual study and weekly group sessions.

Individual study. Each participant will need a *A Woman's Heart: God's Dwelling Place* member book, which contains daily studies to read interspersed with opportunities to respond. Response activities reinforce the readings and encourage personal interaction with the text. Participants will complete each day's reading and writing responses to maxi-mize their learning and personal application of what they learn throughout the study. The member book is divided into an introduction and 10 weeks of content. Each week's material includes five daily lessons, each requiring about 45 minutes to read and respond in the written activities. Participants complete the daily reading and learning activities at home in preparation for the weekly group sessions.

Group sessions. Women meet once a week for 11 weeks for a two-hour group session that guides them to discuss and apply what they have learned during their daily studies at home. In the small-group portion of the session, participants process the material they have studied throughout the week. Small-group sessions build fellowship and rela-tionships, encourage accountability, and multiply the benefits of the study as women learn from the insights of other participants. Women will also draw closer to one another as they share their thoughts, personal experiences, needs, and prayer concerns. Praying together will help them form lasting bonds. In the large-group time women watch weekly video presentations in which Beth Moore speaks directly to the women, enhancing the material in the book and concluding each session with additional truths and challenges.

For women to maximize the benefits of this study, plan for a two-hour group session each week.

To start on time, have child-care workers ready to greet children 15 minutes before each session. Encourage women to arrive during this time and to visit with one another before the session begins. Leadership suggestions in this guide reflect the following schedule:

- Child-care open and workers ready to receive children (15 min. before session)
- All leaders present and ready to greet participants (15 min. before session)
- Large group—welcome, worship, and prayer (15 min.)
- Small groups—prayer (5 min.), discussion of principal questions (20 min.), and discussion of application questions (20 min.) (45 min. total)
- Break and return to large group (5 min.)
- Large group—video presentation (range from 53 to 62 min.), closing assignment, and prayer (5 min.)

This schedule is ideal for a weekday or weeknight study. It may also be used for a discipleship study on Sunday evening if the study begins an hour early and does not interfere with other church activities.

This guide offers suggestions for leading your group. Adapt it to meet the needs of the women in your church and community. Each small-group leader may also adapt the suggestions to her own style or preferences. For example, some leaders may want women to write prayer requests at the beginning of the small-group time and share those requests at the end of the session rather than the beginning. If a group has a tendency to extend sharing and prayer time, beginning the study right away and saving prayer time until the end may help all women get the most benefit from the study.

As you adapt the study's plans to meet the needs of your group, keep in mind the learning styles of both the participants and leaders. This study is not a platform for lectures but a time for participants to share with one another and to learn from one another in a planned format with a leader. Although the plan is flexible, always include: individual home book study, small-group discussion of the principal questions and the application questions in each week's material, and large-group viewing of each week's DVD segment.

CHOOSING LEADERS

If 12 or fewer women participate in the group study, only one leader is needed. The women will form one group and the leader will take on the responsibilities of both the large- and small-group leader. If more women are involved so that you can divide into groups of 10 to 12, you will need a leader for the large group as well as a leader for each small group.

Large-group leader. This leader is organizer, coordinator, and facilitator; her responsibilities include:

- providing administrative leadership
- scheduling the study
- promoting the study
- coordinating enrollment
- enlisting small-group leaders and coordinating their work
- ordering and distributing resources
- leading the weekly large-group sessions

The large-group leader should be interested in exploring the crucial truths of this study and in helping women grow in relationship with God. She should set the example by being faithful in her own study and in her desire to grow in discipleship and in intimacy with God.

Small-group facilitators. These leaders work with 10 to 12 women to guide discussion about each week's session. Responsibilities include:

- staying in contact with and encouraging women in their group

- leading small-group prayer time and praying regularly for participants
- guiding discussion during small-group time
- promoting fellowship
- following up on ministry needs

FACILITATING SMALL-GROUP DISCUSSION

Small-group discussions encourage small-group leaders and participants to apply what they learn to their walks with God and to share insights with one another. Beth applies many of the concepts in her video presentations, and the member book guides participants to apply what they learn as they complete daily assignments. The small-group discussion time each week helps women apply truths to their lives and learn from one another's applications.

Small-group leaders will guide discussions of each week's principal questions listed at the beginning of each week's material in the member book as well as the application questions that appear in the margins of each day's lesson. Small-group leaders can use the following suggestions to facilitate discussion in the small groups.

Before the Session

- Pray for members by name each week.
- Do your homework and think about your group responses to the questions.
- Pray for God to guide you as you facilitate the group.
- Arrange chairs in a circle or semicircle so women can see one another. Seating should include everyone and exclude no one.
- Read Plan A and Plan B each week. You may choose to do Plan A every week. In Plan A you will spend 20 minutes discussing the week's principal questions and 20 minutes discussing key application questions (designated by a heart in the member book). Plan B varies each week and is more activity oriented. You may choose an element of Plan B to enrich plan A, or you may choose Plan B but add to it additional questions from Plan A, or you may choose to use one plan or the other.
- With either plan, be flexible. If women are engaged in meaningful discussion about one question or idea, don't force them to move on just to finish the agenda. On the other hand, don't let one or two women bog down the discussion. If some women seem to disconnect or disengage, move on to the next question or part of the discussion.

During the Session

- Greet members as they arrive and start on time.
- At the beginning or end of the small-group session, allow five minutes for women to share prayer requests and to pray for one another. Pray for women during the week, and encourage them to pray for one another. If needed and appropriate, stop at any time during a session to pray for expressed needs or concerns.
- Encourage voluntary sharing. Invite everyone to participate, but make sure no one feels compelled to share personal information.
- Share some of your thoughts and feelings as a group member. Your job is to facilitate discussion. Occasionally sharing your thoughts and experiences will encourage other women to share and will set a standard for an appropriate level for revealing personal information. While women should be free to share, some may share more than they intend and regret it later. Your example can help women be vulnerable without revealing too many intimate details of their lives.
- Whatever women share, show compassion, concern, and support. Tell what God is doing in your life through this study, and encourage other women to share their own times of real insight and worship during this study.

- Focus the discussion on the lesson's content.
- Listen actively by looking at each woman as she speaks and affirm her for sharing.
- Be prepared to lead a participant to faith in Christ.
- End on time. If women want to continue the discussion, consider exchanging e-mail comments during the week. With participants' permission, collect e-mail address. You can start the discussion by sending an e-mail to participants. Thank them for attending and sharing their insights. E-mail is also a great way to follow up with questions women had during the session that needed research. Encourage them to do their home study every day. If you share discussions online, keep the focus on the previous week's topics rather than the coming week's material. Near the end of each week, just before the next group meeting, you may want to send out a thought-provoking question or teaser for the new session.

After the Session

- Encourage women during the week as needed, and follow up on any ministry needs.
- Pray throughout the week for the Holy Spirit to guide you so that women will get the most out of each session.
- Follow up on any ministry needs.
- Evaluate the session. Think about each woman's participation. Pray for insight and sensitivity to God's Spirit and to women's needs.
- Prepare daily for the next session.

COPING WITH PROBLEMS IN SMALL GROUP

All group leaders face challenges. Difficulties can arise in any group. Here are some ideas for handling some of the most common situations.

Absenteeism. When someone is absent, she misses opportunities for growth and enrichment, and others miss her contributions. When a participant is absent, contact her, show concern, and encourage her to continue her study and to attend the next session. Share interesting insights from the small-group discussion. Tell her she was missed and the group could have benefited from her contributions.

Not completing at-home assignments. Emphasize in the introductory session that a significant course requirement is doing study at home, including completion of learning activities. Explain that daily study is the best way to maximize learning.

Disagreement with content. Although some debate is productive, let Scripture be the final authority. Beth frequently encourages students never to elevate a human teacher above Scripture but to follow the example of the Bereans (Acts 17:11). If debate is extensive or counterproductive, invite the participant to meet with you at another time to continue the discussion and move to the next point or question.

Don't let anyone in the group intimidate, threaten, or bully you. Don't feel you must know all the answers. Offer to research answers to questions the group raises or ask for volunteers to do the research needed to find answers.

A participant who dominates the group by:
- talking only about her own ideas
- waiting until near the end of the session and introducing an emotional or controversial issue
- interrupting and keeping others from talking
- judging rather than accepting what others say
- challenging the leader
- criticizing participants or others

Discourage domineering members by calling on others. Ask those who have not spoken to respond. Speak directly to another woman and ask her to respond. But if subtle attempts to redirect the conversation do not work, speak privately and in person with the offending woman. Sometimes you can enlist the woman's help by explaining that others are not participating. Ask her to help you encourage them to talk.

PLANNING STEPS

The following steps will assist the large-group leader in organizing a study of *A Woman's Heart*.

1. Enlist the support of your pastor. His endorsement will encourage women to see this study as an opportunity to grow in their walk with God, to expand their knowledge of the Bible, and to build fellowship with other women.
2. Talk with women in your church to determine their interest in in-depth Bible study. Take a random poll to discover whether the study should be offered during the day, the evening, or both.
3. Schedule 11 sequential weeks on the church calendar. Consider a weekend retreat just prior to beginning the study. Spring and fall are often the best times for this type study, but plan a time that best fits the schedules of women in your church.
4. Offer child care, if possible. This will make it possible for more women to attend and will reduce absenteeism.
5. Allow two hours for each session.
6. Estimate the number of participants and order member books (*A Woman's Heart: God's Dwelling Place*, item 005076821) for each plus a leader guide (item 005077200) for every large- and small-group leader. Place your order four to six weeks in advance of the study. Decide whether participants will pay for their books. If members pay at least part of the cost of their books, they are more likely to attend faithfully and to complete their home study. If you charge women for the books, arrange for scholarship funds so that cost is not a barrier for anyone who wishes to attend.
7. Reserve the same rooms for large- and small-group meetings for every session. Reserve equipment to show the video study each week.
8. Promote the study—it provides a wonderful opportunity for outreach. Target women in your community who are interested in Bible study. Church bulletins, newsletters, handouts, posters, fliers at Mothers' Day Out, announcements in worship services and in Sunday School classes, phone calls, and word of mouth are excellent and inexpensive ways to promote the study.
9. Pray that God will involve the members He desires and that He will validate this study with His active presence in members' lives.

NOTES

_____

_____

_____

_____

_____

_____

_____

Just Between Us

Because of my love for in-depth Bible study, I have tried to learn what works and what does not work in a women's Bible study. Through the years I have asked many women what they liked and did not like about the way their Bible studies were administered. I have also offered countless evaluations at the conclusions of the studies I have taught. I believe that women are looking for the following characteristics in the administration of their group Bible studies.

Women want organization. When women give the precious resource of their personal time, they must undoubtedly sacrifice something else. They want to know that a program has been well planned and that their time will be used wisely.

Women want the primary emphasis to remain on the Bible study. In other words, during discussion time they are more interested in what God has to say and in the other women's responses to His Word than in the haphazard opinions of others. An effective leader should help keep discussions focused on women's responses to God's Word.

Women want well-respected guidelines rather than stringent restrictions about who can attend and what they can share. Make the group aware that if guidelines are respected, stringent restrictions are not needed.

Women want to feel connected to their study group. They want to meet other members. They want to know they were missed when they were absent. They want to know they added something when they were present.

As a leader, you can help ensure women receive the utmost from this study by implementing the suggestions you have received in this introduction. In addition, you have the opportunity to witness lives being changed, not the least of which is your own! How can I say this without knowing how this study will be received in your church? Because God's Word changes lives! If a woman dedicates herself to the hours this study requires in God's Word, her life will undoubtedly be transformed. As a leader, be careful not to let your administration of this study eclipse your participation in it. Open God's Word and enjoy it! Walk in faith toward the woman He has designed for you to become. His Word will not return void.

Adopt the following verse with me as your watchword and encouragement in leadership. If you fight feelings of inadequacy as I do, memorize these words: "Finish the work, so that your eager willingness to do it may be matched by your completion of it, according to your means. For if the willingness is there, the gift is acceptable according to what one has, not according to what he does not have" (2 Cor. 8:11-12).

9

Small Group Sessions

Broken Hearts, Broken Ties

Before the Session

1. Pray for group members.
2. Complete your work in the member book.
3. Provide name tags, extra member books, paper, Bibles, pens/pencils, as needed.

PLAN A

Review the week's questions (45 min.)

Principal Questions

1. Why were the Israelites to build the tabernacle?
2. What is the human heart like apart from fellowship with God?
3. How did God respond to what He saw at the tower of Babel?
4. What did God preach to Abraham?
5. By what name did God tell Moses to call Him to the Israelites?

Personal Discussion Questions

1. Second Corinthians 5:18 records a beautiful definition of what the tabernacle in the wilderness represented. What has God given us?

2. What does Matthew 6:21 tell you about God's heart?
3. Have you truly accepted that Christ died not only for you but also instead of you? ❑ yes ❑ no If so, explain what that means to you.
4. Think of a time when you cooperated with God by denying your will and following His leadership. How were you blessed through this experience?
5. Can you think of a promise you really wanted to keep—meant to keep—but were unable to? Now, what specific promise has God made to you that He tenderly and faithfully kept?

PLAN B

Preparing Enrichment Activities

1. Provide a whiteboard, flipchart, or chalkboard.
2. Cut out paper hearts for all participants.

During the Session

1. Discuss the meaning of the word *tabernacle* and its purpose. Compare and contrast *tabernacle* and *sanctuary*. Where does God dwell today?
2. Write the word *Reconciliation* on a whiteboard, flipchart, or chalkboard. Discuss with the group: What happened among humankind that made reconciliation necessary? How did the tabernacle play a part in reconciliation?
3. Ask women to look in their purses for something they treasure and, because they treasure it,

carry with them all the time. Women may share photographs or other small treasures.

4. Read Exodus 19:3-6. Point out that God chose people to be His special treasure.

5. Invite women to look through their member books and Bibles to find verses they read last week that show how much God values human beings and His relationship with them.

6. Distribute the paper hearts. Brainstorm what participants learned about the heart in their study this week.

7. Read Luke 2:19,51. Note that Mary's heart was full of Jesus and experiences related to Him. In groups of three or four, talk about what is in the human heart and specifically what each woman holds in her heart. In the small groups discuss whether the human heart is always reliable.

8. With women back together, ask volunteers to share some special comments from their discussion.

9. Invite individuals to write on one side of her paper heart, "My Heart," to reflect privately about what is in her heart, and to write her reflections using symbols indicating whether the things are good and true, whether they are deceptive and misleading, whether they are of God, and so forth.

10. Invite them to turn the hearts over and to write, "God's Heart," with her own name and the reference Matthew 6:21 below.

11. Take prayer requests. Pray for concerns voiced and for each woman to turn her heart toward God.

Just Between Us

Getting started is often the hardest part of any worthwhile task. Do not worry if you encountered a few unexpected challenges or if everything did not proceed as you planned. Celebrate the fact that because of your willingness to be used by God, the women in your study are on their way to greater intimacy with Him! He who began a good work will complete it (see Phil. 1:6)!

—Beth

SESSION 2
New Starts and Barren Hearts

Before the Session

1. Pray for group members.
2. Complete your work in the member book.
3. Provide name tags, extra member books, paper, Bibles, pens/pencils, as needed.

PLAN A

Review the week's questions (45 min.)

Principal Questions

1. How would you describe the physical surroundings of the wilderness?
2. How did God make the bitter water sweet?
3. What did the Israelites long for in the desert?
4. What lesson did the manna demonstrate?
5. How is Christ clothed in Revelation 19:13?

Personal Discussion Questions

1. Have you ever thought of the impact of your faith on your children's future? What difference can this realization make in your daily walk with God and in your parenting?
2. Has God ever led you to taste your own bitterness? If so, what was the occasion, and how have you allowed Him to sweeten your bitter water?
3. First Corinthians 10:21 describes the impossible task of taking part in the Lord's table and the table of demons. Whose table do you choose and why?
4. What do you think God wants to teach us through Matthew 6:11, a crucial portion of the Lord's Prayer?
5. God revealed Himself to His children through His constant care and provision. He still does. In

what ways has He recently shown you His heart by providing for your needs?

PLAN B

Preparing Enrichment Activities

1. Provide a whiteboard, flipchart, or chalkboard.
2. Provide paper and scissors for women to cut out paper dolls or cut out a chain of three dolls for each person in advance of the session. (Internet sites for grandparents have good instructions if you need them.)

During the Session

1. As women arrive, direct them to small groups of two or three. Instruct them to cut out a paper doll chain with at least three figures, or distribute the paper doll chains you have already cut out. Invite women to think of a circumstance when they felt they were facing or in the middle of one of life's battles. Ask them to write their name on a center figure in their paper doll chain. Who stood with them in battle? Ask them to write those names on the other dolls. Have any of these people prayed for them? Have they ever felt that another person came to help them, to walk alongside them as one sent from God?
2. When everyone has arrived and had a chance to complete the paper doll activity, ask volunteers to tell about support they have had in battle or times they have felt all alone in the wilderness.
3. Move the discussion to sharing times women were aware of God's presence in their lives. Invite women to share a Scripture from this week's study or another treasured Scripture that speaks of God's enduring love and presence, His promises of provision, protection, and presence.
4. Discuss these questions: Who in the Bible is a hero or heroine to the women in this group because of the way they fought a battle? Who is a hero or heroine because they have walked alongside someone else who was in battle or crisis?
5. Discuss: What evidence do you see that many people want to claim Jesus as Savior while holding onto things in the world? Invite volunteers to share any struggles in their own lives.
6. Just for fun: Talk about the meaning of God's provision of manna, but get the women to really think about it by asking, How would you feel about gathering and eating the same food every day for 40 years? Similarly, talk about the clothes in the wilderness by asking, Who would want shoes and clothes that never wore out? Imagine wearing the same thing for 40 years? Probably they didn't change size or gain weight eating manna all those years! How does our abundance reflect on the circumstances of God's people on their wilderness journey? Who should be more appreciative of God's provision—the Israelites or we who have far more than we really need?
7. Ask women to turn over their paper dolls and to write on a center doll the name of someone they know whose life is in crisis. Around that figure write the names of those who are supporting that person. Ask women to consider whether God is calling them to support someone they know who is fighting a battle today.
8. Take prayer requests. Pray for needs voiced and that women will hear God's call to carry the name of Jesus to someone in need of His presence.

Just Between Us

I hope that you experienced a little more godly confidence today in your leadership role. I am praying that you will sense God's good pleasure in you as you lead women into His Word. I am also praying that God will send someone to encourage you and to affirm your leadership this week. You are doing a great job! Listen for God to tell you so!

—Beth

SESSION 3
Prepared Hearts

Before the Session

1. Pray for group members.
2. Complete your work in the member book.
3. Provide name tags, paper, Bibles, pens/pencils, as needed.

PLAN A

Review the week's questions (45 min.)

Principal Questions

1. What happened when the Israelites gave generously?
2. What is the one and only sure foundation?
3. In addition to salvation, with what can we be clothed?
4. With what did God fill Bezalel, and why?
5. Why did God tell Moses to go back down the mountain?

Personal Discussion Questions

1. What is your freewill offering to the construction of Christ's kingdom?
2. Which of your activities will stand the test of the fire? Which will burn up?
3. What clothing did your Savior put on so that you could become righteous (2 Cor. 5:21)?
4. Name a job God gave you that was out of your league. How did you respond? In what ways did God empower you for this task?
5. According to 1 Corinthians 10:1-13, why were "these things" recorded for us (v. 6)? Before we judge the Israelites' sins, what does verse 12 tell us? What is our assurance when temptation strikes?

PLAN B
Preparing Enrichment Activities

1. Provide paper, pens or pencils, and small chocolates.
2. On small pieces of paper, write one of the following: a wedding, a child's birthday party, a backyard barbecue with 20 guests, extended family Christmas at your house, a trip to a resort with your husband's work team. Fold these and put them in a basket for teams to select. You'll need one item for each small group of three or four. If you need more, you may repeat these for more than one small team or add your own examples of things that require preparation.

During the Session

1. As women arrive, direct them to form small groups. Let each group select one piece of paper. Tell them they are to list preparation steps for the item they have chosen.
2. After all the women have arrived and had opportunity to participate, ask each group how many preparation steps they had. Reward the team that had the most steps with chocolate. Invite a response of unusual steps or funny steps. Don't go through all the steps for these events. Give chocolate to everyone.
3. Ask the women if they have ever had to prepare for an event like one of these that seemed overwhelming. Ask how they managed to accomplish the task. Answers may include: Doing it one step at a time. Relying on friends and/or professionals. Finding strength through the Holy Spirit. Learning more about what they needed to do.
4. Ask women if God has ever asked them to do something they didn't feel prepared to do. How did they respond?
5. Transition to continue a discussion begun last week about God's provision in the wilderness. Point out that being prepared may mean living in such a way that resources are available when we feel led of God to give them. Ask them to focus on the abundance of food and clothing we all have to the point of causing weight and storage issues. At the same time, many Americans deal with heavy debt

loads. Discuss: Do you think this is God's plan for Christians in the United States? Do we thank God for our abundance? How do you think God would have us use the abundance He has given us? More shoes or a kingdom purpose? Discuss our abundance in light of the generosity of the freewill offerings the Israelites gave.

6. Ask the women if they can think of people who give sacrificially. Be prepared to provide examples if the women do not name anyone.

7. Point out that preparation includes depending on God's provision and also having the right kind of attitude. Discuss: What kind of attitude did the people have when Moses asked for a freewill offering? Does attitude make a difference? Does this attitude also apply to taking jobs in the church, to ministry inside and outside the church? Even to loving acts for family members?

8. Ask a volunteer to read 2 Corinthians 9:1-11. Compare and contrast Paul's request for freewill offerings with that of Moses. How does Paul's request apply today?

9. Ask a volunteer to read 1 Corinthians 3:12-15. What are some examples of a foundation of wood, hay, and stubble? What are some examples of a foundation of gold, silver, and precious stones? How does the right kind of foundation prepare you to be ready for whatever God calls you to do?

10. Take prayer requests. Pray for voiced needs. Pray that women will prepare their hearts and lives to follow God's call in all areas of their lives.

Just Between Us

I hope that God is filling your heart with anticipation as you begin to penetrate the heart of this study, the building of the Old Testament tabernacle. I am praying that God will grant you a deep passion for His Word, one so contagious that every woman in your group captures it. Do not let your administrative duties keep you from completing your own study and benefiting from the blessings God has in store for you and your group. —Beth

SESSION 4
Hearts Approaching the Altar

Before the Session

1. Pray for group members.
2. Complete your work in the member book.
3. Provide name tags, paper, Bibles, pens/pencils, as needed.

PLAN A

Review the week's questions (45 min.)

Principal Questions

1. What place designed for God to fellowship with His people also had an eastern entrance?
2. What did Aaron do with the blood of the sacrifice?
3. What are the distinctions between the different offerings?
4. Why was the priests' washing so important?
5. What was to be a reminder to the Israelites that God was sovereign in how He had chosen to make Himself approachable?

Personal Discussion Questions

1. Think of a difficulty you are dealing with. Test it according to Henry Blackaby's three questions: Are you under attack from Satan or from your flesh? If you are fighting a battle of the flesh, how can you be victorious? What can you do to ensure that you are camped close to your Commander?
2. What is your responsibility after God lights the fire in you (2 Tim. 1:6-8)?
3. You may be surprised and even disappointed to learn that sacrifice was acceptable only on the basis of the graphic procedures examined in this

week's study. What was God trying to teach by demanding such sacrifices?

4. Recall a time when your "pitcher" was empty. How did you feel when others asked you for something during this period of time? How was your pitcher finally refilled?

5. Read Psalm 84. What does it mean to enjoy God's presence and to worship Him intimately?

PLAN B

Preparing Enrichment Activities

1. Display a bowl and pitcher. Have water in the pitcher. Provide a towel.

During the Session

1. As women enter, ask them to join a small group. Their assignment is to talk about gates. What is the purpose of a gate? Is it to keep something or someone in or something or someone out? What real gates have they experienced in life? What symbolic gates have they experienced?

2. When all have arrived and had opportunity to talk about gates, transition to the tabernacle gate discussed in this week's study. Lead women to compare and contrast the gates in their own lives with the tabernacle gate.

3. Talk about the altar and sacrifices. Discuss using question like these: What is the purpose of an altar in churches today? How does it compare with the tabernacle altar? Who can approach an altar in today's churches? Who could approach the tabernacle altar? Why has this changed? What offerings did God desire in tabernacle worship? What offerings does God desire today?

4. Read Malachi 3:7-10. Discuss: In what ways do you think contemporary worship and offerings please God? In what ways is He not pleased with contemporary worship and offerings?

5. Transition to a discussion of sacrifice. What was the meaning of Old Testament sacrifice? Why do

you think God required such sacrifices? What is the meaning of *sacrifice* in worship today? Do you know anyone who lives a sacrificial life?

6. Discuss the cleansing of the priests in this week's study. Was the purpose simply physical cleanliness? What other meaning might the ritual cleansing have had?

7. Read 1 Corinthians 11:28. In what ways do people today attempt to cleanse or examine themselves? Or do they? Why is self-examination important?

8. Pour some water from the pitcher to the bowl. Point out that pure water is a valuable resource in the world today, perhaps another thing many of us don't appreciate fully. Pure water symbolizes cleanliness. Baptism symbolizes our cleansing from our sins.

9. Take prayer requests.

10. Invite women to come forward silently to dip their hands in the water. In this act they should recall their baptism and the cleansing they felt when God forgave them of their sins when they accepted Jesus Christ as Lord and Savior of their lives. Today's act should also symbolize their continuing desire to live a holy life before God as they continue to repent of their sins and seek His forgiveness.

11. When women have returned to their seats, pray for needs voiced. Pray that women will continually approach the altar of their hearts, seeking God's presence and worshiping Him.

Just Between Us

By this time you may have lost a few members. If this has occurred, do not be discouraged or assume that you have done something wrong. Instead, contact absentees to learn how you can encourage them before they reach the point of dropping out. Praise the women who are faithfully attending and completing their home study. You are also to be commended for your commitment to lead this study!

—Beth

SESSION 5
Hearts in Fellowship

Before the Session
1. Pray for group members.
2. Complete your work in the member book.
3. Provide name tags, paper, Bibles, pens/pencils, as needed.

PLAN A

Review the week's questions (45 min.)

Principal Questions
1. What was woven in the fine linen ceiling?
2. What happened to Aaron's rod?
3. Who did Christ send to fuel us so we can be His light in a dark world?
4. How often was the bread to appear on the table?
5. By what name did Christ refer to Himself in John 6:32?

Personal Discussion Questions
1. What would you like to share from your prayer acknowledging God as your caregiver and thanking Him for covering you with His wings?
2. How has the Holy Spirit recently made Himself known in your life through one of these six attributes: wisdom, understanding, counsel, might, knowledge, and fear?
3. Can you identify the fruit of the Spirit in your life? If not, what changes need to occur for your life to exhibit the fruit of the Spirit?
4. From one of God's perfect promises in Isaiah 49:14-16, what phrase tells you something about God's hands?
5. Do you find the bread of Christ's presence satisfying in your life? Why or why not?

PLAN B

Preparing Enrichment Activities
1. Gather large boxes. Stack them at random near the entrance to the door of the meeting room so that it is difficult for women to enter the room and sit down without moving the boxes.
2. Provide felt-tip markers.

During the Session
1. As women enter, ask them to partner with one or two other women to think of barriers they must overcome to have open, growing fellowship with God and with one another. Ask them to write their responses in big letters on the boxes and to stack them against the wall.
2. When all the women have arrived, compare getting through barriers to have a better relationship with God and others to moving through the curtain to get to the holy place. Discuss: What was the purpose of the curtain in the tabernacle? Who could enter the holy place? When have you felt God's presence? When have you felt a special relationship with another person that you felt was part of God's plan? Did you have to overcome barriers to have this experience? What were they? How did you overcome them?
3. Ask women to describe the lampstand. What was its significance? Discuss the concept of light in the Bible. Who is the light of the world (John 8:12)? What is the source of light for your journey through life (Ps. 119:105)? What is the Christian's role (Matt. 5:14)? Who brought God's light into your life? Whose life has benefited because you have brought the light of Christ to it?
4. Ask women to recall a family meal that was almost unbearable because of family tension or a meal that was awkward because they were seated among people they didn't know. Contrast that to a comfortable family dinner where everyone is sharing the events of the day or a church dinner

where everyone is visiting and talking together. Compare both this fellowship and the lack of fellowship over a meal with the tabernacle table and fellowship with God.

5. Read Luke 24:13-35. Where was Jesus revealed to the Emmaus disciples? How do we experience Christ around the Lord's Supper table today? How do these compare to the tabernacle table?

6. Take prayer requests. Pray for concerns voiced. Pray that women will be the light of the world, reflecting the light of Christ wherever they go.

Just Between Us

I hope that you are gaining great pleasure from seeing relationships form and deepen among the participants. Have you seen any results of spiritual growth, such as expressions of ministry?

Ask God to give you a supernatural love for each woman and a deep desire to be a servant leader. Prayer can affect your enthusiasm and willingness to serve in any capacity!

You have arrived at the halfway point of the study. I knew you could do it!
—Beth

SESSION 6
The Heart of a Servant

Before the Session

1. Pray for group members.
2. Complete your work in the member book.
3. Provide name tags, paper, Bibles, pens/pencils, as needed.

PLAN A

Review the week's questions (45 min.)

Principal Questions

1. What duty was performed once a year at the altar of incense?
2. What did Nadab and Abihu offer before the Lord?
3. How did God respond to the actions of the Levites?
4. What did God call the Levites in regard to the priests?
5. What garments were made for Aaron?

Personal Discussion Questions

1. Can you see any results of prayerlessness in your life? Name them. What do you need to do to make prayer a greater priority each day?
2. What fuels your personal expression of worship? Can you sense when God is pleased with your worship, and if so, how?
3. When have you ministered recently as an act of obedience to God? What were the results?
4. Do you have a support system within your ministry? in your personal life? If so, who are they and how do they support you?
5. What attributes of God show Him as a God of individuality?

PLAN B

Preparing Enrichment Activities

1. Consider burning incense or a scented candle during this session. If it bothers anyone's allergies, don't do it! If you know that some of the women in your group have allergies, consider burning a candle with no fragrance. Surround the candle with enough smooth stones to have one for every participant. You can use stones from a craft store or garden center.
2. Display items that give support: a belt, suspenders, support hose, shoe inserts with arch supports, and so forth.
3. Provide small chocolates.

During the Session

1. As women arrive, ask them to discuss in small groups what the items shown have in common.

2. After all have arrived, let them shout out answers until they guess that the items all give support. Reward the whole group with chocolate! Point out that you will talk about support later in this session.

3. If you began the study with a retreat, many of the women may have taken the senses nature walk. Ask women to discuss in small groups ways they have experienced God through their senses.

4. Invite women to share special experiences in which they used their senses to experience God through His creation.

5. What was the purpose of the incense in the tabernacle? Does worship today have a fragrance? Can a fragrance draw you into worshiping God? How would you describe fragrant worship?

6. Discuss prayers of intercession. What have Scriptures you have read this week said about intercessory prayer? Who intercedes on behalf of all Christians? Who prays for you? For whom do you pray?

7. How are worship and obedience related? If your children say they love you and at the same time disobey you, how convinced are you of their sincerity at that time? Do you still love your children? Compare your own experiences as a parent with worshiping and obeying God. Does God still love you when you are disobedient?

8. What does the Bible say about holiness? What does it mean to worship God in spirit and in truth? What does it mean in your church's corporate worship? What does it mean to you in your personal, private worship?

9. Day 4 of this week's study talks about supporting priests. Discuss what the women learned from this section. How does supporting priests in the Old Testament compare to supporting pastors and church staff today?

10. Everyone needs support. Ask women: Who supports you? Whom do you support?

11. Discuss the garments worn by the priests, including the ephod.

12. Take prayer requests. Ask women to pray in twos or threes for needs voiced and to intercede on behalf of others in their group. Before they pray, instruct them to leave silently, taking one stone with them as they leave. Let the stone remind them that they, too, are set apart to obey and serve God and to intercede for one another.

Just Between Us

I pray that you are already beginning to see lives change as a result of time spent in God's Word. Be assured that if you have completed your at-home assignments each week and have led other women to seek intimacy with God, your life is changing too. If you have also seen personal difficulties arise during this time, do not be discouraged. These are opportunities to live what God has taught you in this study. Through all of your experiences He wants to make you living proof that His Word still works. Be ready to receive His instruction and blessing and to share with the group what He is doing in your life.　　—Beth

SESSION 7
A Heart That Intercedes

Before the Session

1. Pray for group members.
2. Complete your work in the member book.
3. Provide name tags, paper, Bibles, pens/pencils, as needed.

PLAN A

Review the week's questions (45 min.)

Principal Questions

1. Why did God impose concrete qualifications on His priests?
2. What was the basis on which the next "Melchizedek" would be named?
3. How was Christ's priesthood superior to Aaron's?
4. What will be different about the new covenant?
5. What is one major way God reveals sonship to us?

Personal Discussion Questions

1. What can you do to offer sacrifices to God in these areas? Praise (for example, giving God glory in all things); Your "temple" (for example, avoiding overwork); and Faith (for example, not giving up when the outcome is not what you wanted)?
2. God chose you in Christ "before the foundation of the world" (Eph. 1:4) and knew you before you were born (see Ps. 139). Has this study encouraged you to feel differently about God's plan or His timing for your life? If yes, explain how.
3. Can you cite a time when you narrowly escaped a sin that could have ruined your life? If it is extremely personal, answer vaguely. The important point is to acknowledge the One who opened before you a way of escape.
4. Think of a past personal need that God undoubtedly and pointedly met in Christ—perhaps the need for acceptance, intimacy, approval, a friend, someone you could trust, or someone to fill a terrible void left by loss. How did God obviously meet this need in Christ?
5. Recall a time when God disciplined you. Why did He? Name at least two different reasons based on Hebrews 12:1-13.

PLAN B

Preparing Enrichment Activities

1. Make a poster with the word *Sacrifice,* or write it on a chalkboard or whiteboard. Before women arrive, place it on a wall where everyone can see it.
2. Secure a chalkboard and chalk or a whiteboard and dry-erase markers.
3. Download a free image of Christ at the door knocking. (Go to Google Images and type in the search space: Jesus door.) You can print this and put it on a poster or project the image.
4. Option: Secure a copy of Beth Moore's *Further Still* (Nashville: Broadman & Holman, 2004). Be prepared to read "Lesson with a Hairbrush," beginning on page 95.

During the Session

1. As women arrive, direct them to gather in small groups and talk about the meaning of the word *sacrifice.* They may want to use questions like these to guide their thinking: What does *sacrifice* mean in our world today? Have you ever sacrificed anything? For whom? Why? Have you ever sacrificed something for God?
2. When all have arrived and had opportunity to join the discussion, ask volunteers to read Romans 12:1-2. What does this passage say we need to do in order to make ourselves pleasing sacrifices to God? Practically, what are some real-life examples?
3. Ask a volunteer to read 1 Peter 2:5. How is it possible for believers today to become a living sacrifice? Whose example are we following? How can we live out being a living sacrifice through our worship?
4. Ask women to name the jobs of a priest described this week. List these on the chalkboard or whiteboard. Since Christians are to be ministers and priests to one another, how can Christ followers today fulfill each of these roles?
5. Transition to talking about the open door from day 3. Show the picture of Jesus at the door, knocking. Point out that "door" like "gate" is a powerful image in the Bible. Ask volunteers to read Matthew 7:7-8; Luke 12:35-36; Acts 12:11-16; Revelation 3:20. Note that Matthew

7 talks about praying and believing, and Acts 12 talks about people praying, having their prayers answered, and having a difficult time believing. Luke 12 talks about being prepared to serve the master. How can women today be ready to serve in opening the door for someone else to meet Jesus or to serve in His name? (Answers may include making time available for ministry, praying that God will make you sensitive to His will for your life each day, saving money to help when a need arises or to go on a mission trip as God directs, and so forth.)

6. Point out that God doesn't always call us to do big things. Sometimes it is a very small but perhaps difficult task. Ask women if God has ever led them to do a small but difficult task. Read Beth Moore's "Lesson with a Hairbrush."

7. Close this session by asking volunteers to say what it means to them to be children of God.

8. Take prayer requests. Pray for needs voiced. Pray for women to be obedient children who do what their God asks them to do.

Just Between Us

I hope that our study of the priesthood has deepened your understanding of the ways Christ serves us and calls us to serve others. Thank you for accepting this challenge to serve Him. I pray that your life will never be the same. —Beth

SESSION 8
Hearts Beyond the Veil

Before the Session

1. Pray for group members.
2. Complete your work in the member book.
3. Provide name tags, paper, Bibles, pens/pencils, as needed.

PLAN A

Review the week's questions (45 min.)

Principal Questions

1. What important task did the cherubim have in Genesis 3:23-24?
2. What might have been the significance of the cube-shaped room?
3. By what authority do you dare enter the holy of holies?
4. What was the significance of the mercy seat?
5. What was the posture of the angelic creatures in Ezekiel 1:11?

Personal Discussion Questions

1. What personal words do verses 7-18 of 2 Corinthians 3 speak to you and how?
2. Which of the Scriptures in the activity on page 168 most nearly addresses your circumstances right now and why?
3. Think back on either your initial salvation or your restoration to God after a time of wandering. How did God draw you to Himself?
4. Think of times you have acted on your own impulses rather than seeking direction from God's Word. What should your plan of action be when you have decisions to make?
5. What new appreciation does your study give you for Christ's words in Matthew 26:53-54?

PLAN B

Preparing Enrichment Activities

1. Gather masks to display.
2. Secure a chalkboard and chalk or a whiteboard and dry-erase markers.
3. Serve hot coffee or iced tea as a symbol of women meeting for a friendly chat.

During the Session

1. Direct women to gather in small groups and to list things women do to hide their true selves.

2. When everyone has arrived, ask them to share some things women do to mask who they really are. List these on a chalkboard or whiteboard. Ask what types of things women want to hide and what kinds of images women want to project.

3. Discuss what it means to be intimate with God. Ask them to brainstorm ideas while you write them on the board. Ask them to consider whether it is reassuring or unsettling that God knows their thoughts, their motives, and all about them—their true selves. Ask how they feel with a close friend who knows all their flaws and loves them anyway. Compare that to intimacy with God. How does this week's study shed light on this concept?

4. Ask women favorite places for hanging out with their best friends. Transition to asking them where they feel closest to God. Where have they experienced God intimately? Where do they have their quiet time?

5. Divide into four groups. Assign each of the groups one of these attributes of Jesus: servant, man, king, God. Ask them to list characteristics of Jesus from their assigned perspective. Then ask how we should be like Him in emulating those characteristics.

6. Take prayer requests. Invite women to volunteer to pray aloud for needs expressed. Close the prayer time interceding for women to enjoy a more intimate relationship with God in Christ.

Just Between Us

I pray that as surely as you have entered the holy of holies in our study, you have entered the holy of holies with God. As you experience deeper intimacy with Him, I pray that He is becoming increasingly irresistible to you. Have you already realized that you could never tolerate living outside the depths of God's Word? If so, praise His name! He has already accomplished an incomparable work in you!

—Beth

SESSION 9
The Heart of the Testimony

Before the Session

1. Pray for group members.
2. Complete your work in the member book.
3. Provide name tags, paper, Bibles, pens/pencils, as needed.

PLAN A

Review the week's questions (45 min.)

Principal Questions

1. What does Isaiah 64:6 say about our righteousness?
2. What is God's foremost instrument for cleaning and pruning us (John 15:3)?
3. What happened to the first set of the Ten Commandments (Deut. 9:1–10:5)?
4. How did Moses respond to the people's obedience?
5. What was the first action God commanded to be done after the tabernacle was completely furnished and why?

Personal Discussion Questions

1. No matter what your background is, you have reason to be thankful that you no longer bear the burden of your sins. We could name pages of things for which we could thank God for His sacrifice and forgiveness through Christ. What five things would be at the top of your list?

2. Reflect on the maturing process through which God is taking you. What lesson did you learn the hard way that you could have learned far more easily by heeding God's Word?

3. Are you are obeying all of the Ten Commandments, or just the ones you find convenient? Ask God to reveal areas of your life in which you have strayed from His laws.

4. Do you find it difficult to persist in a task until it is finished? What is God's guarantee for you in Galatians 6:9?

5. According to Paul's testimony in 1 Corinthians 2:1-2, what were the only things Paul claimed to know? Just as the tabernacle found its acceptance ultimately in the cross of Christ, you have found complete acceptance on the same unfailing grounds. Recall your salvation experience and describe your excitement in knowing that He is present with you.

PLAN B

Preparing Enrichment Activities

1. Make a poster with the word *No!* or write it on a chalkboard or whiteboard.
2. Display garden shears.
3. Provide small Post-it® notes for each person.
4. Make posters with the following words: Work, Home and Family, Personal, Time Wasters, Church and Community Service

Hang them around the room so participants can get to them easily. You may want to have additional poster board so women can divide categories or add another heading for how they spend their time.

During the Session

1. Give each woman a pad of Post-it® notes as she arrives. Ask participants to write one thing that consumes their time on each piece of paper and to place them on a designated wall. (They will move these to posters later.)
2. Then direct them to gather in small groups and discuss the following (you may want to write these questions on the board): Name a job you have done in church, ministry, or community service that was completely draining to you and one that was fulfilling, energizing, and rewarding. What did these experiences tell you about your giftedness? What did you learn about the kinds of jobs you should seek to do and those you should decline? Recall a time when you said no and were glad and a time when you said yes and regretted it.

3. Ask for volunteers to share some examples from their small-group discussion.

4. Ask women what they learned about the Ten Commandments in this week's study. Ask how they feel when they read this list of 10 rules God gave His people. Then lead them to discuss what they learned about the mercy seat from their study this week. Ask them to talk about their own experience of feeling cleansed from their sin, forgiven, or reconciled to God. How do these items, plus the manna contained in the ark, reflect all of God's plan for redemption through Jesus Christ?

5. Invite women to think about what they would like to do in and for the kingdom of God if they had time. List their responses on the board. Hearing responses will prompt others to think of what they would like to do.

6. Ask women to move their Post-it® notes around the posters. Talk about the ways women spend their lives. Which category has lots of notes? Which has only a few? Ask women where they could save an hour or two each week or month to do a ministry they feel led to do.

7. Point out that finding time for ministry is one way of disciplining themselves. We all need to cut out something less important to do something God wants us to do at this point in our lives. This might even mean cutting out one ministry task in order to do another one, if that is what God is leading them to do. Then ask them what other patterns, behaviors, or habits God might want to prune from women's lives to make them more productive in His kingdom. Keep this discussion

general. Then give women a moment to think privately about their own lives.

8. Take prayer requests. Invite a volunteer to pray for needs expressed. Close the prayer time by asking God to give women a vision and passion for serving Him and the desire to allow God to prune their lives in order to serve Him more fully.

Just Between Us

The tabernacle structure is complete, and God's presence is complete. Your work as the leader of this study is also nearly finished, but God's work in you and the participants is eternal. Thank Him in advance for the ongoing work He will do through this study. The last session is crucial. Our encounter with God in the Old Testament tabernacle must now be transformed to a challenge to the New Testament believer. Spend extra time with God this week. He will give you the words to bring this experience to a close.
—Beth

SESSION 10
Mended Hearts, Eternal Ties

Before the Session

1. Pray for group members.
2. Complete your work in the member book.
3. Provide name tags, paper, Bibles, pens/pencils, as needed.

PLAN A

Review the week's questions (45 min.)

Principal Questions

1. How did God intervene and save the lives of Joshua and Caleb?
2. What did the people do "throughout the lifetime of Joshua"?

3. Who is the true Tabernacle?
4. What does the New Testament tell us about God's tabernacle in this present period of time?
5. In the Gospels, how many were invited into the innermost chambers of Christ's glory?

Personal Discussion Questions

1. Has fear ever kept you from walking through a door God obviously opened for you? What have you learned to help you the next time God opens a door?
2. What do you think 1 Samuel 3:19 says about Samuel's ability to speak for the Lord? How does your life reflect your viability as God's spokesperson?
3. What does it mean to you that Jesus had the power to escape His circumstances but chose to endure suffering for our sake?
4. Has it been difficult for you to look in the mirror and accept that you are "fearfully and wonderfully made" (Ps. 139:14)? Why or why not?
5. What it would mean for you to dwell in the holy of holies?

PLAN B

Preparing Enrichment Activities

1. Display a variety of items used throughout the session.
2. Option: create a slide show of free images from the Internet showing Moses, the tabernacle, the wilderness, and so forth. If you do this, have it running as women arrive.

During the Session

1. As women arrive, direct them to small groups of two to four. Ask them to talk about what they have learned from this study. Ask what they expected the study to entail. Invite them to look back at their goals from the retreat and the intro-

ductory session and to determine whether they have met their goals.

2. When all have arrived and had opportunity to participate in a small group, ask them to share some of their reflections about the study.

3. Lead a discussion of what they have learned from studying the tabernacle about God's plan for salvation and how that plan is fulfilled in the New Testament. List parallels on the board.

4. Transition to a discussion of the women themselves as tabernacles, the place where the Holy Spirit dwells. Invite women to recall verses about this in any of the weeks' study. (Let them turn through their member books if needed.)

5. Ask women what hope or promise they find as they read in Revelation about a new dwelling place for God that sounds in many ways like the tabernacle they have been studying. (Listen for responses such as God's consistency, promise of heaven, and hope of eternal life with God.)

6. Distribute paper and pens or pencils or ask women who have kept a journal to open it to a new page. Ask women to reflect on their personal applications of Scripture throughout this study. In light of their own time with God and in light of what Scripture has said to them, what goals do they have for continuing to apply these truths to their lives? Ask volunteers to share one goal they have as a result of this study.

7. Take prayer requests. Ask women to pray with a partner to continue to grow in their walk with God and in Christlikeness. Each pair may choose how much to reveal of their personal goals. After this shared prayer, pray for needs expressed. Thank God for the women in this group and for what He has revealed through His Word. Pray for women to walk with Jesus, continually growing in deeper intimacy with Him.

Just Between Us

How I wish that I could talk with you at this moment to express my deep gratitude for your commitment to completing this journey. You have been an instrument through which God has invited and encouraged women to come and meet with Him. There is no greater calling. Third John 4 says, "I have no greater joy than to hear that my children are walking in the truth." The "children" in your group have walked in the truth because you have led them into the holy of holies! May you forever enjoy the ultimate reward for faithfulness: fellowship with your God. Praise be to Him!

Beth Moore

Video Guide Answers

Introductory Session

1. wonder, pursuit, Where are you?
2. beauty, consistency; verses, devoted, object; caused to see; copy, heavenly, exhibit, imitation, sketch, tracing
3. glory, Son; open, mind

Session 1

1. tree, river, mountain
2. serve, wilderness; walking back, forth, presence, tabernacle; work, care, Eden, tabernacle; naked, crafty
3. visible earth, visible heavens, dwelling of God

Session 2

1. expecting, unexpected
2. daily relationship;
3. daily, pride, fear

Session 3

1. affectability
2. friendship
3. Presence, anxiety; with; significance
4. glory

Session 4

1. awe
2. relief; cover, reconciliation, sacrifice;
3. refuge
4. joy

Session 5

1. echo, Eden, Garden of Eden; cherubim, bar, God's presence
2. branches, buds, blossoms; time, springtime, summer; harvest; all at once, time
3. almond flowers, watch, watchful, vigilant; earliest
4. combined imagery
5. tend, continually

Session 6

sacrifice; prayer
1. blamelessness; have no
2. Gabriel
3. afraid, prayer, heard
4. Lord, done this for me

Session 7

save, uttermost, liveth, intercession
Part 1
protect, heal, whole; all, completion, definite, goal, purpose; utterly, quite; at all, completely
Part 2
will; reflections, first stage, thought, final; spiritual gifts

Session 8

1. anchor, veil; promise; oath, confirmed
2. invitation; confidence, authorization, access; new, living, similar, different, freshly killed, freshness, revelation

Session 9

1. preparation; obedience, exactly; finish
2. filling; rest, abide; *shekinah*
3. transfer
4. departure; inner; threshold; east gate; mountain east
5. Herod's; glory, Israel
6. return

Session 10

Solomon's Temple; Christ; Believers' Temples
Part 1
The Tabernacle, cloud, filled, fire; The temple, filled, glory; The church, heaven, filled, fire, filled; tabernacle, temple, church, temple
Part 2
finished; shape (cube), material (gold); final temple; Eden

A Woman's Heart Retreat

If your schedule allows, plan a women's retreat to launch this study. The plan outline below begins with supper on Friday evening and ends just before lunch on Saturday, but you can adapt the plan and the schedule to fit your needs. Ideally the retreat will not be far from home so that women do not have to drive a great distance, taking a long time to travel to and from the retreat. The goal is to get women away from their routine for a time of worship and fellowship, to spend time with God and with other women.

Pray as you plan. Adapt these ideas and schedule to meet the needs of women in your church and your community.

You can have a retreat—and a women's study group for *A Woman's Heart*—regardless of whether your group is large or small. All size groups have benefits. Women in a small group can get to know all members and form a strong team for future study and ministry. Women in a large group can find fellowship, plan dynamic worship, and reach out to more women in the church and community. Never let the size of your group limit your study, outreach, fellowship, or ministry.

If your group is small, consider using this retreat and study as an outreach even to invite women from the community. Or partner with another small church in your community to do the study. This partnership will enrich women's relationships and may lead to future ministry together.

ENLISTING LEADERS

Women who help plan an event often benefit more from it, are more committed to the retreat and to the study, and are more outgoing in developing relationships at the retreat and during the study because of their ownership in the event. For these reasons, enlist as many women as possible to serve on committees for the retreat. Some possible committees and their responsibilities follow, but keep in mind that these are only suggestions that will get many women involved. A few women in a smaller church can easily adapt this plan and carry out this retreat.

Enlist a coordinator for each major planning area. Each coordinator may want to enlist a committee to work with her on her assignments. Conduct regular planning meetings to make sure everyone is on task, and you will improve the likelihood of a successful retreat. In your first meeting read through the retreat plan. Agree on who has responsibility for each portion of the retreat. During regular planning meetings, review your schedule and plan to make sure all details are covered.

Smaller groups can enlist fewer people to plan the retreat and combine responsibilities. Remember, involve as many women as possible so they will feel ownership of the retreat and study.

Prayer and Retreat Coordinators

Prayer is an important element of any retreat and study. Every step should be an object of prayer. The prayer coordinator should be involved in all meetings so that she knows details and any concerns. Pray for God to lead you in all details concerning the retreat and for those who will participate in it.

1. Choose a committee of persons who will commit to pray for every aspect of the retreat.
2. Before the retreat pray for the planning details and each coordinator by name.
3. Decide on the dates and location for the retreat. This retreat can be done on a Friday night through Saturday or on Saturday only. Options for possible retreat settings include a retreat center, camp, lodge, or any location away from everyday distractions. Another option is to hold this retreat at your church.
4. Plan regular meetings with the coordinators to discuss plans and get updates on how each committee is progressing. Work with the administration coordinator to determine a schedule for the retreat.
5. Be available to help coordinators accomplish their tasks and to encourage them along the way.
6. View the introductory session on the DVD ahead of time.
7. The prayer coordinator will prepare and lead women in their nature walk/sensory prayer time or enlist others to do this.

Music Coordinator

1. Work with the prayer coordinator to plan music that will lead participants in praise and worship.
2. Enlist musicians.

3. Make arrangements for sound equipment, musical instruments, and any desired PowerPoint visuals. Be certain items such as choruses, lyrics, and announcements can be easily read when they are projected.

Administration Coordinator

1. Work with the retreat coordinator to determine location and fee. Keep in mind expenses for food, lodging, conference rooms, copies of *A Woman's Heart* for all participants, fabric and other retreat supplies such as arts and crafts items, and expenses and gifts for outside singers or musicians.
2. Record all planning and meeting decisions.
3. Keep account of finances.
4. Work with the promotion coordinator to conduct registration.
5. Order a member book for every participant. Include this cost in the total cost for the retreat.
6. Order *A Woman's Heart Leader Kit* with DVDs to show the introductory session during the retreat.
7. Arrange for access to a DVD player and a large monitor so that participants can easily view the session.
8. Option: order a model of the tabernacle for participants to construct during an optional activity time. Models are available at a number of Web sites.
9. Option: arrange to have bookmarks made on colorful cardstock as an encouragement to women to complete the Bible study (p. 32). Coordinate with colors used in the retreat fabrics and name tags if desired.

Small-Group Coordinator

1. Pray for small-group leaders.
2. Lead small-group leaders to select the fabric— quilt, tapestry, woven scarf, and so forth—to bring to the retreat, and be prepared to tell about it in the context of sharing about the fabric of their own lives.

Decorations Coordinator

1. Decorate tables with fabrics of scarlet, blue, and purple.
2. Provide candles and matches for each table.
3. Make a gift bag for each participant. Include *A Woman's Heart* member book, a small notebook to use as a journal, a pen, tissues, and fruit.

Promotion Coordinator

1. Promote the retreat with brochures, signs, and announcements, providing all necessary information. Use the promotional video segment to advertise the study and the retreat.
2. Work with the administration coordinator to conduct registration. Send a letter to all participants about the retreat. Include driving directions to the retreat location, the time the retreat will begin, and items the women will need to bring.
3. Set up a registration table at the retreat location before participants arrive. Give attendees name tags, pieces of fabric, and gift bags.
4. Direct women to small groups to begin interviewing each other.

Food Coordinator/Hostess

1. Plan for meals and snacks during the retreat.

RETREAT SCHEDULE

Before the Retreat

1. Designate a wall inside the building but preferably outside your primary meeting area as The Great Barriers Wall.
2. Prepare an equal number of blue, purple, and scarlet name tags. Prepare twice as many pieces of fabric in the same colors, cutting them approximately three by five inches (two pieces of the same color per person). Use these fabric pieces to divide women into groups. If you are using only one schedule for the study, you may want to use these colors to divide the women into their small groups for the entire study. You can combine or divide color groups to get approximately 10-12 in each group. Fabric need not be rich, expensive, or even the same for an entire group. It just needs to have a dominant color of blue, purple, or scarlet. It can be brocade or gingham, felt or cotton print. You may want to invite women to contribute remnants they have or purchase inexpensive remnants in the designated colors.
3. Option: order a model of the tabernacle to be constructed. Models are available at a number of Internet Web sites.
4. Provide measuring tapes and tape or some other kind of markers for women to measure off the dimensions of the tabernacle. Enlist someone to lead this optional activity.
5. Place candles and matches on each table for dinner, but do not light the candles until the worship service begins.
6. In advance of the Friday evening worship service, make sure some women are prepared to begin a song or speak a Scripture. You may want to ask small-group leaders and the worship team to take the lead as needed.
7. Provide art materials such as paper, chalk, pens, pencils, crayons, and modeling clay.
8. Ask women to bring flashlights if you are meeting in a state park or an area where they can take a nighttime nature walk.
9. Each small-group leader will need to bring a large piece of fabric with multiple colors or pieces of fabric, or a woven piece with different colors of yarn. Examples include quilts, rugs, tapestries, and scarves.
10. Enlist one or two women to share a brief testimony about an encounter with God.
11. Enlist one or two women to share a brief testimony about their growth as a result of another in-depth Bible study.

FRIDAY EVENING

1. As women arrive, provide nametags. Give each woman two pieces of fabric that match the color on her name tag—blue, purple, or scarlet.

2. Give each woman a small pad of Post-it® notes and a pen or pencil. Invite her to think about the barriers she had to overcome to find time to come to this retreat, the barriers she will have to overcome to do the daily work for this study, the barriers she will have to overcome to attend weekly sessions, and the barriers in her daily life to a closer relationship with God. Ask each woman to write one barrier per Post-it® note and to place it on The Great Barriers Wall.

3. After women have completed writing their barriers, ask them to partner with one or two other women with the same color name tag, preferably women whom they do not know well. Ask them to interview each other so they can introduce one other person to the group. After their interviews, ask them to pray for one another—that their personal barriers will not interfere with their thoughts during the retreat, that God will help them overcome all barriers, that God would defeat Satan's attempt to distract them from focusing on this study, and that they would develop a closer relationship with God over the coming weeks. The women may want to share contact information and become prayer partners during the study.

4. Ask women to eat dinner sitting with women with the same color name tags and fabric. At some point before, during, or after dinner, let women introduce one another briefly, telling at least one new thing she learned about the woman she interviewed.

5. After dinner move to a time of worship. You may do this around the dinner tables or move to another meeting room. This worship time is informal and participatory, so the seating arrangement is unimportant.

6. Let the large-group leader briefly introduce the study. Explain that while women are learning about the tabernacle in the Old Testament, God's first dwelling place among His people, they will also be examining their own hearts and their relationship with God. This is appropriate since they, as Christ's followers, are the dwelling place of the Holy Spirit. As they grow in knowledge about God's Word, they will also grow in their relationship with Jesus Christ, God's Son.

7. Explain the plan for worship will be a service led by participants. Instruct the women to sit silently, praying and listening for God. At first, they may feel uncomfortable in the silence, but expectant waiting and worship can be powerful in hearing God speak to them. As they feel led, they may speak a Scripture, sing a hymn or chorus, or offer a brief praise to God. Other women may join in the singing if they choose. Women should not worry about reciting Scripture perfectly or giving chapter and verse if they cannot recall it. They should not be distracted by finding the words to a hymn or looking up a verse in their Bibles. Their speaking and singing should be spontaneous acts of praise and worship, sharing with God and this community of faith words of Scripture or song that have been meaningful in their faith journey.

8. Signal the beginning of worship by asking women to light the candles on their tables. As women are doing this, dim or extinguish lights in the room.

9. Continue the worship service for 20-30 minutes or longer if women seem comfortable and are participating. Remember to dwell peacefully in the silence and stillness, allowing God to speak.

10. Bring worship to a close by standing and inviting women to quietly sing a familiar praise chorus.

11. Announce the time for breakfast. Tell women they will need their Bibles and their piece of fabric in the morning. Announce optional late-night and early-bird activities. Tell women that they are dismissed, but provide activities for women who want to continue fellowship.

12. Optional activities for late-night and early-bird activities include these:

- Build a model of the tabernacle using the kit(s) ordered from the Internet.
- Measure indoors or outdoors the size of the tabernacle. Someone will need to be prepared to lead this activity, either by having the dimensions researched and ready or by leading women to find the measurements in their Bibles.
- Express praise creatively. Display art supplies and invite women to create something that symbolizes their relationship to God, an attribute of God, or something that symbolizes their worship.
- Take a prayer walk. Some may want to do this in the evening, in the morning, or both. As they walk, ask them to reflect on God in creation by using all their senses to experience God's creation. What do they see? What do they smell? What do they hear? What do they touch? What have they tasted during the day? As they walk, suggest that they thank God for the things they see, hear, smell, feel, and taste.
- Write in their journals about their experiences in worship and anything they heard from God during that quiet time.

SATURDAY MORNING

1. Provide art resources, tabernacle model, measuring tools for marking the size of the tabernacle, and instructions for a prayer walk (see information in 12, optional activities) in the meeting room where women can find them. Provide a poster to remind them of the time for breakfast.

2. Breakfast

3. After breakfast invite women to take their fabric pieces and go alone to a quiet place with their journal and Bible to think about the fabric of their lives. Give them instructions (p. 32) and a time and place to join their small group, designated by the color of their fabric.

Small-Group Time

1. Display the special piece of fabric so that it is clearly visible when women enter the room.

2. Remind women that this is a study of the tabernacle, the first place God dwelled among His people. It was built by His instructions. He chose the size, the items to be used in worshiping Him, the colors, and the fixtures.

3. Explain that today as well as in the Old Testament people met God in many different places, but the tabernacle was a special place of worship for meeting God. It was so special that only designated people could enter the tabernacle at appointed times. Today Christians not only have ready access to God because of the Holy Spirit dwelling within, but we are also privileged to worship in God's house throughout the week and throughout the year.

4. Invite women to share some of the times they have encountered God.

5. Ask women to partner with one or two others and describe the fabric of their lives.

6. Tell about the piece of fabric you brought. Point out that part of what makes it beautiful is the variety of colors, fabrics, threads, and so forth. The beauty is a unique combination of texture, color, cloth, and the skill of the one who created it. Each woman present was created in God's image to be a unique person with distinct characteristics, experiences, and gifts. And all of these wonderful women come together to bring what they have to combine with others to make a rich tapestry of God's special people.

7. Call women in the small group together and distribute member books for *A Woman's Heart: God's Dwelling Place*. Ask them to talk about their expectations and goals for the study. Note that women who set goals for completing the study and anticipate learning more about God's Word and drawing closer to Him will benefit more from the study.

Break

1. Ask small-group leaders to display their quilts, rugs, and other special fabrics in the front of the large-group room so the women can see them when they enter the room.

Large-Group Time

1. Plan for a time of prayer, singing, and testimonies. Singing can be *a cappella* choruses or familiar hymns; a solo, duet, or trio from previously enlisted participants; or a guest singer from outside the church. Have previously-enlisted women share testimonies of their experiences of meeting God or their experience in a previous in-depth Bible study.
2. Introduce the study by telling about Beth Moore and some of her other studies.

3. Show the introductory video.
4. Remind women about the times and places they will be meeting.
5. Encourage them to be committed not only to attending weekly sessions and to doing their homework but most importantly to growing in their knowledge of and relationship with God.
6. Offer a time of invitation in which women will bring, as a sign of their desire to grow in discipleship, one of the pieces of their fabric to a designated spot at the front of the room. Ask them to place the other piece of fabric in their Bibles as a reminder of their commitment.
7. Dismiss to return home.
8. Consider taking the fabrics women have brought to the altar and letting a creative woman make something of the fabric that can be displayed where the women will meet for the study.

"Finish the work, so that your eager willingness to do it may be matched by your completion of it, according to your means. For if the willingness is there, the gift is acceptable according to what one has, not according to what he does not have."
Second Corinthians 8:11-12, NIV

The Fabric of a Woman's Life

1. If your life were a fabric, what colors would you see? Would there be one color or many colors? What would they represent?

2. What kind of cloth would it be—rich brocade or plain cotton, smooth or textured, clean and new or tattered and torn?

3. What would be the use of the fabric? Would it be decorative or functional, as a table runner or a bath towel? Would it be stationary or mobile, such as a sofa or a warm coat?

4. In the fabric of your life, recall the places where you have met God. What colors and fabrics would represent those experiences? Where were you? What time of year and time of day was it? What were the circumstances of your life at that time? How did you feel? What color comes to mind to represent this experience?

"Finish the work, so that your eager willingness to do it may be matched by your completion of it, according to your means. For if the willingness is there, the gift is acceptable according to what one has, not according to what he does not have."

II Corinthians 8:11-12, NIV